# Investigations

# Sliding

## Patricia Whitehouse

Heinemann Library
Chicago, Illinois

© 2003 Heinemann Library
a division of Reed Elsevier Inc.
Chicago, Illinois

Customer Service  888-454-2279
Visit our website at www.heinemannlibrary.com

Designed by Sue Emerson, Heinemann Library; Page layout by Que-Net Media
Printed and bound in the United States by Lake Book Manufacturing, Inc.
Photo research by Beth Chisholm

07 06 05 04 03
10 9 8 7 6 5 4 3 2 1

**Library of Congress Cataloging-in-Publication Data**
Whitehouse, Patricia, 1958-
  Sliding / Patricia Whitehouse.
      p. cm. – (Investigations)
Includes index.
Summary: Presents simple hands-on experiments that demonstrate the properties that make sliding easier or more difficult.
  ISBN 1-4034-0906-4 (HC), 1-4034-3471-9 (Pbk.)
  1.  Friction–Juvenile literature. 2.  Surfaces (Physics)–Juvenile literature. 3.  Friction–Experiments–Juvenile literature.
  4.  Surfaces (Physics)–Experiments–Juvenile literature. [1. Friction. 2. Friction–Experiments. 3. Experiments.]  I. Title.
  QC197 .W45 2003
  531'.6–dc21

                                        2002014426

**Acknowledgments**
The author and publishers are grateful to the following for permission to reproduce copyright material:
pp. 4, 6, 7, 8, 9, 10, 11, 12, 13, 14, 15, 16, 17, 18, 19, 20, 21, 22, 23, 24, back cover Que-Net/Heinemann Library; p. 5 Mug Shots/Corbis

Cover photograph by Que-Net/Heinemann Library

Special thanks to our advisory panel for their help in the preparation of this book:

Alice Bethke,
Library Consultant
Palo Alto, CA

Eileen Day,
Preschool Teacher
Chicago, IL

Kathleen Gilbert,
Second Grade Teacher
Round Rock, TX

Sandra Gilbert,
Library Media Specialist
Fiest Elementary School
Houston, TX

Jan Gobeille, Kindergarten Teacher
Garfield Elementary
Oakland, CA

Angela Leeper,
Educational Consultant
North Carolina Department
of Public Instruction
Wake Forest, NC

Some words are shown in bold, **like this.**
You can find them in the picture glossary on page 23.

# Contents

# What Is Sliding?

Sliding is a way of moving.

You are sliding when you go down a slide.

Some places are good for sliding.

Some places are not.

# Is a Hard or Soft Place Better for Sliding?

ice

Put a **brick** on some ice.

Gently push the brick.

The brick slides on the hard ice.

The ice is a good place for sliding.

Put the **brick** in some sand.

Can it slide now?

The brick gets stuck in the soft sand.

The sand is not a good place
for sliding.

# Can Something Smooth or Rough Slide Better?

This hard floor is **smooth**.

Socks are smooth, too.

The socks and the floor are
both smooth.

They can slide against each other.

These shoes are **rough** on
the bottom.

Can they slide on the **smooth** floor?

Rough things cannot slide well on a smooth place.

# Can You Change Something from Rough to Smooth?

The heavy jug is **smooth**.

Can it slide on the **rough** wood?

Gently push the jug on the wood.

It does not slide.

Pour some dish soap on the wood.

Now what happens when you push the jug?

The jug slides.

Soap makes the **rough** wood **slippery**.

# How Can Water Help You Slide?

Your swimsuit is **smooth,** and the dry plastic is smooth.

Can you slide?

You can slide on the plastic, but not very far.

Spray water on the plastic.

Water makes the plastic **slippery**.

Slippery places are good for sliding.

Now you can slide!

# Quiz

Which is a more **slippery** place?

Look for the answer on page 24.

# Picture Glossary

**brick**
pages 6, 7, 8, 9

**rough**
pages 12, 13, 14, 17

**slippery**
pages 17, 20, 21, 22

**smooth**
pages 10, 11, 12, 13, 14, 18

# Note to Parents and Teachers

Through play, children examine the physical world and various forces of nature that affect it. This book extends child's play into experiments about the physics of friction. These experiments explore whether two surfaces will slide against each other or not. The experiments use materials that can be found around the home and classroom, so children can repeat an experiment they read about.

Each chapter looks at the characteristics of two surfaces and how these surfaces may interact. Read each chapter, repeat the experiment, and talk about what you have learned. For example, after reading pages 10 and 11, have children slide across a smooth floor in their socks. Then read pages 12 and 13, and have the children try sliding across the floor with their shoes on. Ask the children to think of other places they might slide, such as down a slide or on ice, and how sliding in those places is like sliding on the floor in their socks.

**!** CAUTION: Children should not attempt any experiment without an adult's permission and help.

# Index

**Answer to quiz on page 22**

The wet, soapy floor is a **slippery** place. Be careful!

24